ROLLING...
IN-LINE !

Long strides help a competitive
skater reach top speed.

ROLLING... IN-LINE!

by Larry Dane Brimner

A FIRST BOOK
FRANKLIN WATTS
New York / Chicago / London / Toronto / Sydney

*For the kids in schools in Davis, California,
who suggested it — Happy Rolling!*

Readers should remember that all sports carry a certain amount of risk. To reduce that risk while in-line skating, skate at your own level, wear all safety equipment, and use care and common sense. The author and publisher will take no responsibility or liability for injuries resulting from the use of in-line stakes.

Cover photograph copyright © Jack Geschiedt

Photographs copyright © : Jack Geschiedt: frontispiece, pp. 6, 10, 20, 22, 26, 28, 30, 47, 50, 51, 57; The National Museum of Roller Skating: p. 9; Mark Doolittle/ Outside Images: pp. 13, 15, 17, 23, 40, 43, 44, 53, 54; Michael Dwyer: p. 58.

Library of Congress Cataloging-in-Publication Data

Brimner, Larry Dane
Rolling—in-line! / by Larry Dane Brimner.
p. cm. — (First books)
Includes bibliographical references and index.
ISBN 0-531-20171-6
1. In-line skating—Juvenile literature. I. Title. II. Series.
GV859.73. B75 1994
796.2'1— dc20   93-51255 CIP AC

CONTENTS

Bicycle paths are popular with in-line skaters.

HOW IT ALL BEGAN

Wheels! Ever since these circular devices were invented, people have been busy thinking up new ways to use them. One newfangled approach to this age-old invention is to use them by rolling on your own feet—in-line! In-line skating is something new, but surprisingly, it has a long history. In 1760 Joseph Merlin hatched the idea of attaching wooden spools to the soles of his shoes. His goal was to provide a means of "ice skating" in warm weather. Voilà!—he skated. And there wasn't a sheet of ice in sight. The wooden spools, however, proved impractical as warm-weather ice skates because they didn't lend themselves to turning—or stopping.

For years, Merlin's invention was forgotten. Then, in the early 1800s, another ice skater tried putting wheels on shoes. Robert John Tyers of London placed five wheels all in a line on each shoe. The device, which he called a "rolito," worked, but most people considered it a folly. However, in 1863, James L. Plimpton of New York came along and mounted a pair of wheels in front and another pair in back. By cushioning the wheels on rubber pads for easier turning, he made the skates more maneuverable and grew wealthy as people happily picked up the sport of roller skating.

Tyers's idea of in-line wheels never completely faded from the picture, though. In the Netherlands, a few ice skaters began to use a primitive form of in-line skates, called "skeelers," on dry land after the ice had melted. Still, the idea of in-line skates didn't really catch on.

Then in 1980, two brothers from Minnesota discovered a pair of the primitive in-line skates while rummaging through a sporting goods store in the Midwest. Scott and Brennan Olson thought the design would make a good off-season hockey training tool and borrowed on the idea to produce a pair with greater maneuverability and speed. Their idea was to market the new skates to hockey players who wanted to practice during off-season. With padded boots made from synthetic materials and polyurethane wheels, the new in-line skates performed much like ice skates. Only stopping was different. For that, the Olsons attached a brake pad to the heel of the right skate. Christening their newly formed company Rollerblade, Inc., they assembled the skates in the basement of their parents' home.

*A primitive in-line skate similar to this
one sparked the Olsons' imagination.*

The new in-line skates proved popular, but hockey players weren't the only ones interested in the Olsons' skates. Skiers found that they duplicated many of the techniques of skiing, so they began to use them. Soon, other athletes began to use them for practice and exercise, too.

During the 1980s the popularity of in-line skating began to grow, and "blades," as in-line skates are sometimes called, began to be seen along trendy California beaches. People who had never become skilled on ice skates or traditional roller skates found that in-line skates provided greater ankle support, and they quickly learned how to "blade" (skate).

Today, with more than six million enthusiasts, in-line skating is the fastest-growing sport in America. Professional in-line skate troupes travel worldwide to skate, dance, and perform stunts. Racing events are springing up everywhere; and for the first time, 1992 saw in-line skaters competing in the World Speed Championships in Rome, Italy. It seems that no matter where you look—whether it be out your window or simply at television—you'll find people rolling . . . in-line!

In competition, this in-line skater attempts to clear the high jump bar.

CHOOSING THE RIGHT IN-LINE SKATES

Any athlete's success depends, in part, upon the quality of the sporting equipment used. Inferior equipment makes superior performance difficult, if not impossible, to achieve. Before deciding on one particular brand or style of in-line skates, you should first ask yourself how you plan to use them.

Each in-line skate consists of an outer boot, or shell; an inner boot, or liner; a frame, or chassis, that attaches the wheels to the boot; and the wheels themselves. The shell is usually made of polyurethane or some other plastic, or of leather, or a combination of the two. How stiff it is will depend on the kind of material from which it is made. If the shells of the skates you buy are too flexible, you won't get the ankle support that beginners often need. Also, be sure that your boots can "breathe." If there is no air circulation within the boots, sweaty feet can become uncomfortable and irri-

Some in-line skaters "adjust" the fit of their skates with duct tape.

tated. Look for vents. Skating is no fun if you have blisters on your feet!

Inside the boot is a padded liner that provides comfort by absorbing jolts and jars. Besides providing comfort, liners also give your feet greater stability. The more stable you are in your skates, the better able you will be to control their movement and direction.

If your feet are still growing, look for boots that can accommodate liners of more than one size. Liners can be bought separately, and you'll get more wear out of your skates if you can replace an outgrown liner. That should make your parents smile.

Speed skaters and those wishing to perform stunts will want frames of rigid construction. Quality skates have frames made of reinforced nylon, aluminum, or an alloy that offers strength. To test frame quality, turn the skate over. Grip the frame at each end and try twisting it. It should give only a little. The frames on less expensive skates have more flex and offer less stability and control.

Wheels are rated by size (diameter) and hardness (durometer). The larger the wheel, the faster the ride. Young beginners will likely use skates with wheels that are 64 mm in diameter. Most adult beginners should use wheels from 70 to 72 mm in diameter. On the

Five-wheeled skates
are designed for speed.

other hand, skaters interested in competitive racing may use wheels as large as 80 mm.

Whether to skate on hard or soft wheels is up to the individual skater. A wheel's hardness is determined by its durometer rating; the higher the number, the harder the wheel. Rollerblade, Inc., equips most of its in-line skates with wheels having a durometer rating of between 88A (recreational) and 78A (racing). Softer wheels tend to grip the pavement better and provide more shock absorption. They also enable better acceleration, which is important to racers. While harder wheels give a faster ride on a smooth surface, such as the wood floor of an indoor rink, they may slide on pavement outdoors. Because outside factors—temperature and skating surface, to name two—will influence the performance of your wheels, it's best to experiment. Generally speaking, wheels in the durometer range of 88A to 78A will be adequate for most skaters.

Whether to choose skates having three, four, or five wheels is another consideration. In certain instances, you may have no control over the number of wheels on your skates. In-line skates with three wheels, for example, are designed for smaller feet! For people with larger feet, the four-wheeled variety will meet most skating needs—recreational, hockey, and artistic.

Freestyle skaters push their limits and impress crowds by "getting vertical."

Beginners should avoid five-wheeled skates, though, as they're intended for racing and serious training. The longer wheelbase (the distance between the center of the front axle and the center of the rear axle) of five-wheeled skates provides longer strides, or rolls, and the added stability necessary at higher speeds.

Several manufacturers are now in the business of making in-line skates. As a result, prices vary greatly, ranging from $59 to more than $400. You needn't bankrupt yourself for a decent pair, though, which should run around $200 to $300.

Beware the bargain! Cheap skates can sometimes lead to thrills, the kind you want to avoid. Because they are often constructed of inferior parts and materials, they sometimes don't provide a skater with adequate support and control. An out-of-control skater is a hazard not only to self, but also to others. Also, cheap skates may prove more costly in the long run as parts will likely have to be replaced frequently.

If you can't decide which in-line skate is best for you, consider renting them in the beginning. This will give you a chance to experiment with different brands and models. But most rental shops require a deposit, just in case the skates are lost or stolen. You'll want to take along an adult, because deposits can be as expensive as the skates themselves.

AVOIDING INJURIES

Just about any pastime more active than chess involves some risk of injury. Because in-line skating involves speed and movement, it is no exception. But savvy bladers know that by wearing the correct protective equipment, the risk of injury can be minimized. In-line skaters should always don their protective gear. Rollerblade, Inc., puts it this way: "Don't skate naked."

Because you'll want to get as quick a start as possible, it's best to buy your protective equipment as soon as you buy your in-line skates. You'll need wrist guards, knee and elbow pads, and a helmet.

The most common injury to bladers is sprained or broken wrists from pitching forward during a fall. Wrist guards with hard plastic inserts not only help support your wrists, should you go down, but they also protect your palms from "road rash," or scraping. Velcro fasteners allow for a snug fit. Prices range from about $20 to $40.

Knee and elbow pads usually have foam padding and plastic cups to absorb the shock of impact. While some styles are elastic and slip on, others come with Velcro fasteners. The choice is yours, though knee pads using Velcro are more handy should you forget and put on your skates first. Expect to pay between $20 and $40.

Injuries to the head are the most dangerous. **Never skate without a helmet.** Some in-line skating manufacturers are marketing their own lines of helmets, but you'll likely find a larger selection of styles and models at a bicycle shop. Whichever helmet you select, be sure that it meets the American National Standards Institute's safety guidelines for bicycle helmets. The helmet's label will carry the initials ANSI or SNELL if it does. Prices start at around $35.

If street hockey is your in-line sport of choice, then you'll need some extra safety gear. These include shin pads, padded hockey gloves, hip pads, and a face-screened helmet that meets Canadian Hockey Standards.

In addition to the add-on equipment, in-line skates that fit properly will also help you to avoid injuries

A young skater takes to the pavement with lots of padding, but what's missing?
Never skate without a helmet.

Ramp stunts like this require practice and skill, but you should never skate beyond your ability level.

A street hockey player prepares to score. Note his gloves and shin pads, an added precaution to guard against injury.

because they'll give you more control. When you try on your skates for the first time, remember to wear cotton sport socks. In-line skates should be snug, but not too tight. While you stand with your knees unbent, your toes should just barely touch the front of the liner. Bending your knees and squatting should then cause your toes to pull back from the front of the liner. The fit shouldn't restrict your toes; you should be able to give them a wiggle. Most of all, your in-line skates should be comfortable. If they are not, you'll end up not using them—and miss out on a treat!

Of course, a good fit and safety equipment alone can't guarantee an injury-free session of blading. Attitude is equally important to avoiding injury. Skate smart. Be rested when you practice; fatigue can lead to accidents. And don't attempt to skate beyond your confidence and skill levels. To build those, learn the proper blading technique.

4

BLADING BASICS

If your first strides on a pair of in-line skates are shaky, don't let it bother you. Mastery of any skill requires time and practice. With some steadfast effort on your part, you'll be zipping along with rhythm and flow.

After getting into your safety gear, the first thing you'll want to work on is maintaining your balance while standing and moving in your in-line skates. Some people, especially those with ice-skating experience, have no difficulty balancing. For most others, acquiring the knack of standing without toppling requires some practice.

Instead of heading straight for the local velodrome, a first-timer should look for a wide, level, dry patch of lawn. The grass will prevent you from picking up too much momentum and, should you happen to fall, cushion your landing.

ROLLING

The ready position

Practice by taking a "duck walk." With toes pointed outward, take a few walking steps. This is how you'll push off once you're ready to board actual pavement.

If you sense a fall coming—and at some time you will—bend at the knees and waist and drop almost into a racer's crouch to lower your center of gravity. Extend your arms out to the sides, too. This gives you greater balance and puts you closer to the surface if you should actually fall. The secret to a safe landing when you fall is to be wearing *all* of your safety gear. Then try to fall forward so that one or more of your six impact points (two wrist guards, two elbow pads, and two knee pads) absorb the shock. Avoid landing on your rear if you can because the spine is especially sensitive to impact.

There's an easy way to get up after a fall. From a hands-and-knees position, bring one knee up to your chest with your skate opposite the other knee. Put your weight onto the bent leg and push yourself up to a standing position. Ta da! You should be upright and ready to roll.

Skilled skaters, like this one, can expand the basic jump into stalls, grinds, and other impressive maneuvers.

After you get comfortable with the duck walk, try to balance your weight first on one leg, then on the other. This back-and-forth shifting of weight and balance is basic to skating.

Most beginners start to feel comfortable on their in-line skates in no time at all. But everybody learns at a different rate. Move on when *you* are ready, not before.

When you do feel that it's time for something more challenging, find a flat sidewalk, driveway, or parking lot. Either pedestrian or automobile traffic can be hazardous to the beginning blader, so pick a place that is free of interference. Also, look for a location that has no obstacles. Twigs, gravel, cracks, and potholes can throw a blader off balance. Unless you're attempting uncontrolled flight, choose a place with a smooth surface and sweep your path of travel free of twigs and gravel.

To get in the proper skating stance, bend at the knees and waist just as if you were planning to sit down. This slightly crouched position will put your weight on the balls of your feet and give you balance. Remember to keep your weight off your heels; if you don't, you will be thrown off balance.

A skater demonstrates the rear brake stop.

STRIDING

After you feel comfortable in the basic stance, you'll be ready for some self-propelled motion. Skating is really a series of connected pushes and glides, called *striding*. To start, position your feet in the ready position: point one toe outward and the other toe in the direction you want to travel. (This is also called the T-position.)

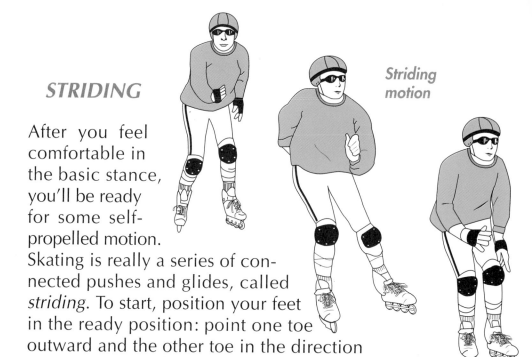

Striding motion

In-line skating appeals to a broad range of people.

The outward-pointing skate should be slightly behind the other skate. Assume the crouched stance, and push off with the rear skate as you shift your weight to your forward leg. Now you should be gliding under your own power. Bravo! Keep your hands low and in front of you to help you balance on one leg.

Next, bring your pushing skate forward until it is parallel to the gliding skate and transfer your weight onto it. Push off with the other skate (the original gliding skate). Voilà! You're in-line skating.

To cover distance, you simply connect together several pushes and glides into a series of strides. Allow your hands to sway from side to side and you'll develop a smooth, side-to-side rhythm.

In the beginning, some bladers have trouble developing a smooth rhythm. Their pushes and glides look choppy. This is probably because they're not getting a forceful enough push-off. They shift their weight too early to the opposing leg. The sequence should be like this: push (right skate), shift weight, glide (left skate),

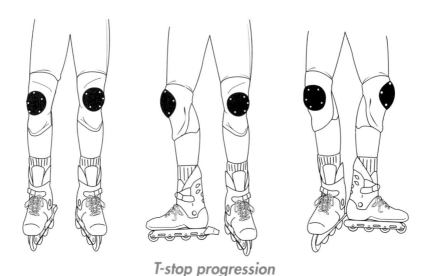

T-stop progression

push (left skate), shift weight, and glide (right skate). From side to side, the motion should blend into a smooth, swaying rhythm—a ballet for wheels.

STOPPING

Once you're in motion, you need to consider how to stop. If there's a grassy area adjacent to your skate path, the easiest way to stop is to roll off the pavement and onto the grass. The grass will slow your momentum and bring you gradually to a stop. Just be sure it isn't soppy wet, or you'll stop more abruptly than you plan and topple in the process.

Because there won't always be a lawn nearby, you're going to want to know how to stop in other ways, too. In-line skates come with a brake mounted on the rear of the right boot. To use the brake, crouch slightly and slide your right foot ahead of your left foot. Bend your left knee and straighten your right leg. While keeping your feet parallel, tilt the forward (right) foot upward and press the brake into the pavement. The more pressure you apply and the more you bend your left knee, the more abrupt will be the stop.

Stopping on in-line skates takes practice. Practice until it's second nature to you. It's smart, too, to start learning how to stop by skating at slow speeds. Once you can perform a controlled stop without thinking about it, you can add more speed.

You may notice that some in-line skaters use alternate methods of stopping from time to time. One alternate method is the T-stop, which gets its name from the formation of the skates when doing this maneuver. To perform the T-stop, place your right foot perpendicular to and behind the left one with your right toes pointed outward. Bend both legs slightly and drag the right skate forward toward the heel of the left boot. Bending your right foot so that all of the wheels come in contact with the pavement, press down to stop.

The disadvantage of using the T-stop is that it wears out your wheels quickly. A heel brake costs only around $5 to replace. A new set of wheels can run $50 or more. Be sure to choose a stopping method that will fit your budget.

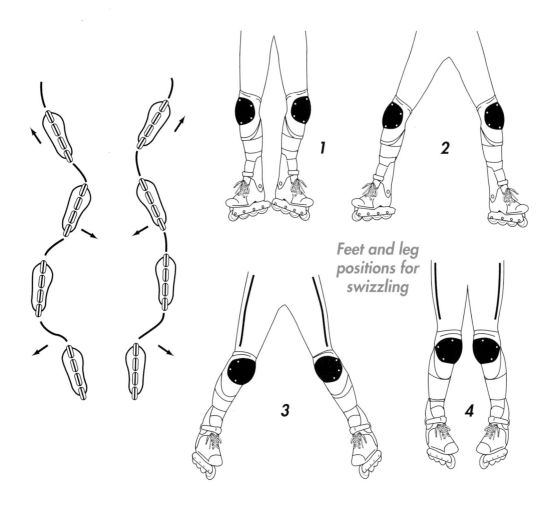

Feet and leg positions for swizzling

The power slide is an impressive stop. Except that you use only one foot, it's similar to an ice hockey stop, minus the ice. This stop begins with a basic rolling technique, called *swizzling* (or sculling). To swizzle, move your legs in and out so that your skates trace the

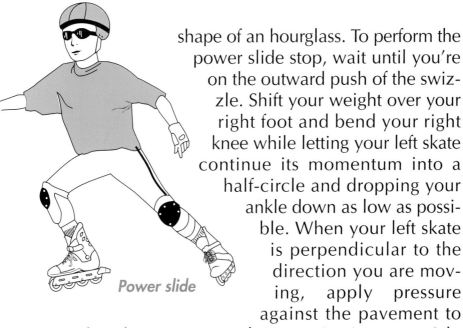
Power slide

shape of an hourglass. To perform the power slide stop, wait until you're on the outward push of the swizzle. Shift your weight over your right foot and bend your right knee while letting your left skate continue its momentum into a half-circle and dropping your ankle down as low as possible. When your left skate is perpendicular to the direction you are moving, apply pressure against the pavement to complete the stop. Remember to maintain your weight over your right foot as you apply pressure.

The disadvantage of the power slide stop is that, like the T-stop, it adds additional wear to your wheels. Also, there's a chance of injuring your ankle or shin, not to mention the possibility of scratching the side of your frame and boot.

TURNING

Eventually, every blader wants to change direction. Turning on blades is similar in technique to turning on skis, and it happens almost by itself. Turns occur by *edging,* or skating on the edges of the skate wheels. To practice edging, start from a forward glide. With your

Basic turning

feet parallel, bend both knees and turn your head and shoulders in the direction you wish to turn. This will cause your skates to angle slightly, and you'll begin to turn in the direction that you're looking. Be sure to practice edging both left and right; if you don't, you'll find yourself going in a circle!

The crossover is a more advanced turning technique, though there's nothing complicated about it. It still relies on edging to accomplish a shift in direction. To accomplish a left turn, look to the left. Bend your left knee as you glide on your left skate and lean slightly toward the left, transferring your weight over the left foot. This will cause you to *edge* on the outside of the left wheels. (The more you lean, the more pronounced the turn will be.) In the leaning position, let the right skate pass across and in front of the left one for the next stroke. Put it down, and glide on the inside edge of the right skate's wheels.

Raise the left skate and bring it forward, crossing the toe of the left skate behind the heel of the right skate. It should be angled so that it comes down on its outside edge. Keep repeating this maneuver to skate in a counterclockwise circle.

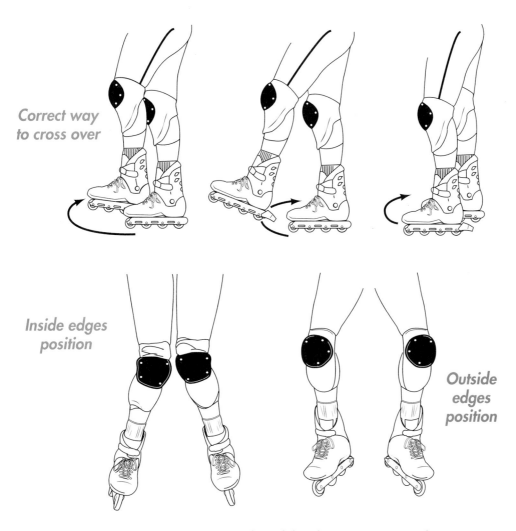

Correct way to cross over

Inside edges position

Outside edges position

Once you feel comfortable skating in one direction, try the other direction. Be sure to spend more time practicing the direction that feels most awkward so that your turning skills will be balanced.

SKATING BACKWARD

To skate in a backward direction, practice backward swizzles. Think about what you want to do, then follow through with the action. Roll slowly at first, building up speed as you gain more confidence.

From the backward swizzle, you can begin to practice the backward stride. As you glide, skates parallel, shift your weight over the push skate and glide on the other skate. Now the glide skate becomes the push skate, so your weight should be concentrated over it. Push. Then glide on the original push skate. Back and forth, over and over, and you'll be striding *backward*.

To turn, look over your shoulder in the direction you wish to travel. (To turn left, look backward over your left shoulder.) Extend your right arm in front and your left arm behind. Concentrate your weight slightly over your left skate. Without lifting it from the pavement, roll the right skate and cross it in front of the left one. When your right skate passes the toe of the left one, shift your weight to the right skate. For a moment, you'll be cross-legged. Lift your left skate, and return it parallel to the right one. Then repeat the maneuver to skate in a clockwise circle.

Skating backward may seem difficult in the beginning, but with practice it will become as natural as skating forward. It just takes time and patience—and perhaps a spill or two!

CHAPTER
5

PEOPLE AND SPORT

In-line skates and the people buckled into them can be found everywhere. Sure, blading has its share of daredevils who push freestyle stunts to their outer limits, but it also attracts serious athletes and the more sedate who simply enjoy a good workout and the sensation of quietly zipping along at a nice clip.

Unlike traditional roller skating, which generally appealed to elementary-school-age children and, for a time during the 1970s, to young adults, in-line skating has crossed over generational barriers to attract people from a broad range of ages. And unlike skateboarding, bicycle racing, and BMX freestyle, in-line skating has also attracted a large number of female enthusiasts. Fully one-third of those participating in in-line skating are female, and their presence is growing.

Families looking for a pleasant and invigorating outing have discovered that in-line skating is something

they can do together. Commuters trying to beat traffic and parking are donning their blades. One commuter, a lawyer in San Diego, California, blades to and from court and "parks" his wheels in his briefcase! Not only does blading beat sitting in traffic; it can provide a good workout and be ecologically correct. And because in-line skating is relatively young, there's plenty of room for beginners to make their competitive mark; there simply aren't many "in-line legends" to compete against—at least, not yet!

Because of in-line skating's connection to ice hockey, it's fitting that one popular blading activity is roller hockey. The Roller Hockey International League made its debut in 1993 with twelve competing teams. These professional teams play on an official roller hockey rink that measures 180 to 200 feet (55–61 m) in length and is 85 feet (26 m) in width. The league plays a regular season of fourteen games, with the top eight teams advancing to the playoffs and winners eventually going on to compete in the finals.

You don't have to be a professional roller hockey player, though, to enjoy the sport. Informal matches are cropping up on outdoor basketball courts and even on city streets, which is why roller hockey is also dubbed "street hockey."

Commuters are discovering that in-line skates offer an alternative to gridlock.

Unlike an ice hockey team, which has six players, a roller hockey team has only five players—two defensemen, two forwards, and a goalie. The rules differ, too. In roller hockey, checking is not allowed. Also, players can move the puck without concern that a teammate is out of position. There is no offside rule. These variations make for a fast-paced game, one in which halves are limited to fifteen minutes.

When space is limited, some street hockey proponents play a one-goal variation of the game, where one team defends the lone goal while the other team tries to score. Once a goal is scored, the teams change positions, attackers becoming defenders and defenders becoming attackers. The first team to score a predetermined number of goals is the victor.

Whether you play at an official rink or at your local cul-de-sac, it's wise to wear safety equipment specially designed for roller hockey. Knee, elbow, and shin pads, and padded hockey gloves are essential. Equally important is a helmet with a face shield. Look for one that meets Canadian Hockey Standards. As defender of the goal, the goalie requires additional armor. A goalie's padding, glove, and arm shield can total around $100, but the payback will come in the form of safety—and blocked pucks.

Street hockey is a fast-moving game.

*A goalie's mask should meet the
Canadian Hockey Standards.*

Roller hockey also calls for other trappings. You'll need a hockey stick. They're usually made of laminated wood and curved either right or left, depending on whether you're right-handed or left-handed. Choose one that just reaches your chin when you stand it upright in front of you.

A roller hockey puck is different from an ice hockey puck. An ice hockey puck is made of hard rubber. In roller hockey the puck is made from weighted plastic so that it will slide smoothly, no matter what the surface. Some players use a "no bounce" roller hockey ball instead of a puck. About the size of tennis balls and much heavier, they are available at sporting goods stores that carry in-line skates and equipment.

Of course, if the game is truly informal—just a group of friends and family—there's no need to spend a lot of money on fancy pucks and sticks. You can have just as lively a game of street hockey with a tennis ball or volleyball. Instead of a hockey stick, you can use an old broom (i.e., with bristles intact). But be ready for a speedy, high-flying game where absolutely anything might happen. After a few of these exciting games, you might want to line up the neighborhood talent and form a league of your own.

FUN AND FITNESS

Are you tired of being a couch spud? In-line skating is ideal for anyone who wants to get fit and stay that way. All you have to do is put your blades on and go. Because blading is fun, you'll be less likely to give it up out of boredom. Everybody knows that the secret to any exercise program is longevity. Stick with it and mushy muscles soon become taut and toned. Even better, you'll be doing your heart and lungs a favor by making them stronger, too.

In-line skating strengthens every muscle, from the lower back to the knees. If you swing your arms vigorously as you skate or skate with ski poles, your upper body will be exercised as well. Also, blading is easy on your knees. Exercise is achieved without the heavy skeletal stress often brought on by running or high-impact aerobics.

By using in-line skates, people can improve their

*In-line dancers get fit and
have fun at the same time.*

endurance and burn body fat in a short time. A thirty-minute workout at a steady, comfortable rate consumes on average about 285 calories. The faster and harder you skate, the more calories you burn. You will also increase your aerobic training—that is, the workout you give your heart and lungs—by skating uphill. Remember, though, that before you skate uphill, you should know how to control your speed when you come downhill. To lose control skating downhill is to risk becoming "bacon in a pan," a term bladers sometimes use to describe a skater who has just slammed the pavement.

Because in-line skating is based on a side-to-side motion, it mimics skiing. For this reason, it is used by the U.S. Ski Team for practice and exercise, or cross training, in the dry months. Bicyclists, speed skaters, rowers, and many other athletes also cross-train on in-line skates.

As you can see, in-line skating isn't just a bonus to hockey players like Wayne Gretzky, an avid blader when he's not on the ice. Anybody can do it—and have fun while getting into better shape.

COMPETITION

If you like speed, in-line racing is a surefire way to catch some thrills. Among the fastest self-propelled athletes in the world, in-line skaters often average speeds of 25 miles (40 km) per hour on level terrain and can race downhill at 55 miles (88.5 km) per hour.

Many racing events are organized by the International In-line Skating Association. But two other organizations, the Outdoor Marathon Rollerskating Association and the United States Amateur Confederation of Roller Skating, also allow in-line skaters to compete in their events.

The most common events are 5 km (3.1 miles) and 10 km (6.2 miles) races. There are also longer competitions. The annual Athens-to-Atlanta (Georgia) race covers an 84-mile (135-km) course, while the Fresno-to-Bakersfield (California) race—said to be the world's longest in-line skating event—is a 138-mile (222-km)

In-line competition is cropping up everywhere.

Winning the slalom requires speed and
dexterity — but this skater is
breaking the **Never skate naked** rule!

journey. The World Speed Championships also now allow in-line skates in all competitive distances, ranging from a 300-m (1,000-ft) timed race to a 20-km (12.5-mile) race.

Five-wheeled skates with low-cut boots make possible the long, rhythmic strides that speed skaters use to reach high gear. A crouched position and stretchy nylon clothing help cut down on wind resistance.

Other competitive events include slalom racing, and the high and long jumps. For those who dare to be artistic, there's dance and freestyle.

Freestyle stunts are being developed at an amazing rate as in-line skaters venture to try more and more daring feats. Many of the tricks are attempted by launching into the air, or, in in-line jargon,"getting vertical." These are usually performed on a half-pipe (ramp). Others are performed on the street. An element common to many of them is the basic jump.

***

You should not try to perform a basic jump—or any stunts, for that matter—until you are a fairly good blader. Here's how to do a basic jump. Approach an obstacle with enough speed to clear it. Base your speed on the height of the obstacle. A taller object requires

A young freestyler tackles the ramp.

more speed than a shorter one. In the beginning, it's best to practice with something short.

Start out by approaching the obstacle in a crouched position. Bring your arms backward to begin the upward momentum. To launch, swing your arms forward and push up with your legs, driving your body upward. As you rise into the air, continue the upward momentum by bringing your knees toward your chest. Then spot your landing point before gravity takes its course.

To land, begin to extend your legs and lower your arms. As you make contact with the ground again, bend your knees to absorb the impact and remain in a crouched position until you have regained control. Use your lowered arms to steady yourself if necessary.

The basic jump can be expanded into other stunts by adding variation. Curb stalls, curb grinds, front-side rail slides, and even grabs have at their heart this essential movement. Using your imagination to create something uniquely your own will impress judges and earn you freestyle points as well.

Freestyle stunts are limited only by the imagination, but complicated moves like this one are not for the novice.

THE LAW AND IN-LINE SKATING

In-line skating is a great way of spending time with friends and family. It gives you a good physical workout at the same time it provides fun. But as the sport becomes more popular, it is facing opposition and restrictions. Some communities are adopting bans on in-line skates just as they have done on skateboards and roller skates.

Many of the objections to in-line skating come from people who have had encounters with inconsiderate or out-of-control bladers. If you zip up behind a senior citizen or dart into traffic, chances are that you'll make enemies, not friends.

Other objections come from the potential for property damage caused by bladers. These concerns are understandable. Some skateboarders performing stunts such as curb grinds and rail slides have torn up property, and people view in-line skaters in the same way.

Individual bladers can best fight negative images

Stunts are best performed on ramps
designed for this purpose.
Be respectful of private property.

by setting a good example. Always skate in control and with courtesy. Be aware of your surroundings to reduce the possibility of mishaps.

Become an in-line ambassador. If you are asked to leave an area, do so. Before leaving, though, politely try to find out what the objections are. Understanding why people are asking you to leave may help you to change their opinions later.

Be informed and always obey the law. One man in St. Louis, Missouri, was caught by the police skating 30 miles (48 km) per hour in a 25-mile (40-km)-per-hour zone. Although lawyers might reasonably argue that speed laws were not created with bladers in mind, a speed law is a speed law, and it should be adhered to regardless of the mode of transportation.

If bans on blading do exist in your neighborhood, you can work to bring about a change. Attend city council meetings. Join or form an in-line skating group. Explain that in-line skating is not only recreation but, for many, also transportation and serious exercise.

If you show people that you are a responsible blader by skating safely and courteously, most will not oppose the sport. In fact, you may even inspire some of them to whiz around on in-line skates themselves.

In-line skating is a quiet way to get in touch with your inner thoughts.

ORGANIZATIONS AND PUBLICATIONS

You may want to know more about the sport of in-line skating. The following list of organizations may help.

International In-Line Skating
   Association
Lake Calhoun Executive Center
3033 Excelsior Boulevard
Minnetonka, MN 55416

National Museum of Roller Skating
4730 South Street
Lincoln, NE 68506

Outdoor Marathon Rollerskating
   Association
P.O. Box 181
Pine Lake, GA 30072

United States Amateur Confederation
  of Roller Skating
P.O. Box 6579
Lincoln, NE 68506

BOOKS

Miller, Liz. *Get Rolling: The Beginner's Guide to In-Line Skating.* Union City, CA: Pix & Points Publishing, 1992.

Rappelfeld, Joel. *The Complete Blader.* New York: St. Martin's Press, 1992.

Sullivan, George. *In-Line Skating: A Complete Guide for Beginners.* New York: Puffin, 1993.

MAGAZINES

In-Line Magazine
2025 Pearl Street
Boulder, CO 80302

Speed Skating Times
2910 N.E. 11th Avenue
Pompano, FL 33064

U.S. Roller Skating
P.O. Box 6579
Lincoln, NE 68506

INDEX

Italicized page numbers indicate illustrations.

ABOUT THE AUTHOR

Larry Dane Brimner is the author of many picture books and nonfiction works for children and young adults. His First Books for Franklin Watts include *Animals That Hibernate, Unusual Friendships: Symbiosis in the Animal World, Karate*, and *Snowboarding*. He is also the author of *Voices from the Camps: Internment of Japanese Americans during World War II*. He lives in Southern California.